WHISPHERS OF MELANCHOLY

VERSES OF DREAD AND DESIRE

JACOB ELDHO GEORGE

Made with ♥ on the Notion Press Platform
www.notionpress.com

Contents

Preface   *v*

Acknowledgements   *vii*

Prologue   *ix*

1. Lost Snow   1

2. The Creed Of Sin   2

3. The Prayer Of The Ashes   3

4. Sworn In Cold   5

5. The Fallen King   8

6. The Ones Above   13

7. The Queen Of Insanity   15

8. The Movements Of Pain   17

9. The Echo Of Regret   19

10. A Facade Of Me   23

11. Unspoken Solace   25

12. The Forsaken One   27

13. When Can I Break   29

14. The Dread Of The Sunrise   32

15. To Those Who Never Rose   34

16. Cradle Of The Humane   36

17. The Truth In Shadow   38

18. Judgement Calls   40

19. Death The Gospel   42

20. Still We Walk   44

Author's notes   47

Contents

Thank You   51

Preface

Within these pages lies the world of my poetry, where my ideals freely dance with the darker elements of life.

My poetic style is built upon placing myself in the shoes of others and personifying the emotions they would have felt in those situations. My poems usually dwell on the themes of loss and sacrifice while placing emphasis on the sinister elements of life. They are not bound by the present or the mundane but instead embody legacies and legends of history or delve headfirst into the philosophical elements of this world.

I have written these poems with a lot of thought and research, and I hope every piece of my poetry is able to paint a vivid image in your mind.
Thank you for joining me on this journey into the world of my dark and gritty poetry.

Also before enter the world of my poetry I would like to mention that because some of my poems may be inspired by some historic tales or may have some complicated methaphors I have included some authors notes for all the poems as a part of the end matter so if you feel inclined to learn more about these poems please do read the end matter at the end of this book

Warm regards,
Jacob Eldho George

Acknowledgements

To my parents, thank you for always motivating me to keep on writing and for teaching me all the ideals that I stand firm on today, and showing me the right path and the right way to do anything and everything.

To my sister, thank you for being my inspiration to start writing poetry and for helping me to find the power of my words. Thank you for all-around being a wonderful sister and helping me through many things, such as my studies.

To my friends, my family, and everyone else who has helped me along the way, thank you for your encouragement, and whether it may be via conversations, shared experiences, or simple words of motivation, thank you for always motivating me.

To the world of anime, history, and legends, you've ignited my creativity, blossomed my imagination, and shown me that stories are not just told they are felt. Thank you for giving me so much inspiration.

And finally, to the readers, thank you for stepping into my world, where even the faintest emotions are felt, where the shadows coexist with light. This book is not just a collection of poems; it is a reflection of my thoughts mended with emotion and illustrated with passion.

May these words resonate with you, and may you find your own meaning within these pages.

Prologue

Here, grounded in these pages
lies a world of my thoughts
born in fire
molded by desire.
Within this world
my emotions run wild and free
mending themselves into verses
crafted in the abyss of my soul.
These pages whisper verses
tainted with sorrow
where dread and desire intertwine
giving birth to the Whispers of Melancholy.

1. Lost Snow

Snow, I know I haven't felt you in a while,
but I still remember how you feel
how you melted away in my arms.
Snow, in this unbroken chain of summers,
the world feels so blistering without you by my side.
Life feels so sorrowful;
even in this spree of smiles,
all I can find is a tear on my face,
crafted from the sorrow of losing you.
Snow, even though you were so cold, you were always my
warmth.
Snow, you were so dazzling,
in your beauty I swayed.
Oh, how your frost warmed my heart.
Snow, in this hellscape of a world,
I only wish to feel your embrace once more.
But it seems I am too late,
as you are already one with the earth.

2. The Creed of Sin

I am sin
the spark of tyranny,
the maze of misery
With my hands bathed in blood,
I linger in your shadow.
For I am a taunting ember
which births a sinner's flame.
I am where the shadows roar,
where broken vows soar.
My actions face no reprimand,
as I forge the lost and damned.
My taunts can grasp
even the purest of saints
for I am not bound by the laws.
I am your fleeting wrath,
your bitter lust,
your slothful pace,
your envious gaze,
and your ambiguous pride.
For I am sin
who finds his creed within your greed.

3. The Prayer of the Ashes

The flames of the liars consumed her whole,
yet her soul remained so pure.
Her hands still formed a prayer,
though met with cruel refrain.
Her lips still parted a litany,
though they tasted the ash.
She, a child who once looked
at saints with golden eyes,
now saw that many saints
only spew lies with their golden tongues.
She fought for many
none fought for her.
Oh, Holy Maiden,
she saw that her path would end in fire,
but she kept on marching through,
no matter the pain or the suffering.
She marched and tread
her path of destiny.
She cried not for herself
but for the comrades she could not save.
Known to pain,
yet unknown to gain.

She carried no sword,
yet her path was carved in blood.
In the fire, they wished to burn away her and her legacy,
but instead, they burned her into history.
As she parts, there is no vengeance
only a prayer for salvation.

4. Sworn in Cold

My blade is born,
My path is sworn.
The thoughtfulness fades,
The heartlessness parades
To me, their screams are nothing but a symphony,
As I am nothing more than tyranny.
My path, stained in blood, still reeks of sorrow.
I reminisce the times when everything was bright.
I close my eyes and try to reach for that moment
once more,
so I can feel the days
when my mates and I would
sit by the lake,
greet the ladies,
flirt with the girls,
and laugh away.
Once more, I reach for those days.
But now, I am lost in a storm of screams,
The lake's echoes fade, replaced by clashing steel.
Oh…
I have no clue where my morals went.
My blade became my soul

I burned my soul to fight, nothing more,
nothing less.
For now, I am nothing but an empty soul,
Fighting for motherland
Or was I?
My ideals, now as dead as my soul,
My yearning for freedom, now just a craving for silence.
In the snow, I've lost myself.
Now, I am just a shadow
of a forgotten time,
My actions remain, but their reasons erode.
It seems…
My heart, once warm,
Now cold and firm.
I feel my senses drown in frost,
No longer can I linger and smile
in the snow.
For all I see is a field of corpses,
Draped in crimson snow.
My veins run cold as my blood seeps out,
Yet I can't escape every path is war.
Every time my blade pierces an enemy,
It pierces my soul.
Now, my hands are bathed in sin,
My soul woven in screams.
For my hands carve their ends, yet stain me in turn.
In the fall of my enemies, I find no peace,

JACOB ELDHO GEORGE

And in my own, I expect none.

5. The Fallen King

The once-immortal king, now a mortal, stands
Atop a hill of countless corpses.
He, who was blessed with forever, a body that would never
bleed—
Yet all of it lost, alongside his hope.
The mighty king, now amidst betrayal,
Remembers his rise
From a simple boy,
Who, by mistake, pulled a sword from stone,
From a nameless child to King of Britain, and the
Lord of faeries, chosen by fate, bound by misery.
Now, standing atop the lives of many,
With his once-immortal body stained in blood,
He wished only for good.
But in his ideals, he lost his soul.
His people, bound by lies, now forge blades
To end him.
A king born of desire,
The embodiment of fire,
He weeps not for the crown he lost,
But for the kingdom that has fallen.
He sees the lands he fought for now lost to wrath,

His blade striking down former comrades.
Now bound to reality, his kingship comes to ruin.
He sees his son the child he abandoned.
Though born of mishap,
No child deserves the fate of loneliness.
Oh, the poor soul, lost in his
Path for fatherly love,
Now met with reality
He sees that no one will love him,
For he was a child born through incestuous misery.
Once a loyal knight bound by his father's ideals,
Now just a lost child,
Who had finally understood he was a mess
Born of lust.
He cries,
Lost in the sea of screams.
Morgaine, in her witch's ways, whispers:
"If Arthur cannot be the father he should be to you, then he
should die."
The words echo through the broken soul
And find their footing.
He, the one who once
Slayed those who betrayed the great king,
Now leads them.
And so, atop a thousand corpses,
The end draws near.
The once-immortal emperor, slain by his own son,

Rises once more
To end his own mistake.
The great King Arthur is no more. What remains
Is a man wounded by the past.
Arthur feels the weight of life
For the first time in ages
Tears, forgotten, return as he feels lost between life and death.
As he stands wounded, his most loyal knight besieges him.
Whilst the knight carries him to safety,
Arthur's eyes are locked upon
The lands of Camelot.
He is enraged by the destruction brought upon by his people.
For he knew that he was to blame for their rage.
He looks for the remains of his chivalrous subjects,
But when he looks, he only sees broken souls,
Hardened by sorrow
The winds of sorrow recite to him the truth:
His blade of light, once a symbol of victory,
Had brought only death.
The people's cries still echo in his mind
Their resentment,
For him,
And their feeling that he was inhuman,
Their screams roaring,
"You failed us,"
Still thunder in the depths of his soul.
As his thoughts linger and the last shreds

Of his godhood fade,
His mentor's memory,
His love, his hate
Sins and mistakes,
All dragged back to him.
the once perfect king now a broken facade
Ah, the mighty king once free of such thoughts,
Now a mere mortal, grounded by them.
As the sights of Camelot hurry away, he tries
To grasp his kingly ambitions once more, but fails,
As the echoes of Camelot fade.
He is put beneath
The guard of a tree,
His heart beckoning questions of why,
Whilst his thoughts try to answer.
At last, his sorrow
Crafts his realization
The error of his rule.
Only a man shaped by pain could ever be a king.
For a leader must understand his people.
With the weight of life pressing him, he feels his regrets
Burn him. He sees that for now, he must fade away.
So he throws his blade to his knight
And pleads him to return it to its rightful place,
The lake where he had received it from Vivian,
The first time he became king.
The knight, torn between loyalty and love,

Tries to change the fallen king's heart,
Knowing the sword's return seals the king's fall.
But seeing it as his king's last wish,
The knight obeys.
He casts the sword into the lake.
And the hand of fate grasps the sword,
And Arthur's fate with it.
With the last piece of his power gone,
Arthur's soul drifts into place, his completion,.
Born by the desire for the end.
He says to his knight,
"Let me drift upon the waters
For I am no king now."
As he begins to give in to his wounds,
Drifting in the lake, he screams:
"A fallen king, I shall rise
When my people call, I will return,
To cut through the darkness so that my
Kingdom may shine bright once more."
As he fades, the fairies carry him,
Even those who loathed him,
Taking the king to Avalon,
Where he shall rest
Until the day when his return is desired,
And his kingdom calls him home.
Though he may not have been perfect,
He was still Britain's once and forever king

6. The Ones Above

The bars of steel that crush my dreams,
The tyrants above that bind me to this path.
They grant us the illusion of choice but puppeteer
us to our end.
Their strings hold us to paths of dread.
In our deaths, they see no meaning,
for all they do is feast upon our cries.
It saddens me.
It enrages me.
My sorrow births my lust for revenge.
My wrath calls upon the chaos within me,
breaking the chains that bound me.
Now, with my eyes no longer groped by their shadows,
I see the path to victory.
I tread this path—
though each step is pain,
but a step closer.
The queens and kings call me a heretic.
They turned my rebellion
into a tale of heresy,
portrayed me
as a man gone mad,

possessed by evil.
Ah, what irony—
the ones drowned in sin brand me as sinful.
I will change this broken world devoid of choice.
I will end this brutality.
I will end the kings and queens.
I will roar, I will scream until my lungs can no longer breathe
about the dream of
a land not bound by royalty.
They hunt me with their bloodthirsty fangs,
take my riches, burn my name, and raze my home.
in their sinful path they carve mountains of corpses
but the cries of those dying souls births the flame of desire
My wrath has become my cause.
I walk only for my ideals.
I will destroy this despotism.
I will pave the way to a land of the free.
Though I may not reach it,
I walk with the hope my people may.
As I see my brothers raise their voices,
I realize they may have caught me, but the next will rise.
I lay my head to the flames, for I know that my brothers
will hear my cry for freedom and take a step from where I fell.
So let me fall and fade into echoes of time,
for I have found my purpose as the spark of rebellion.
So let my blood fuel their way to a land of the free,
a land of truth and a land of equals.

7. The Queen of Insanity

Though her body
screams ordinary,
with hints of beauty
her thoughts were
of mischief,
and cruelty unknown to this realm.
She wears a façade,
a mask of calm
so none may flinch,
so none may see.
Oh, how easily
men are tricked
by her daunting beauty,
only to witness
the true nightmare of desire.
her eyes take no setour
always looming on the results of her massacre
She, a child forgotten by the light,
a shadow of sinners' screams.
She forsakes the sane
and chooses instead
to be devoured

in chaos and brutality.
Her beauty, a mere façade.
She, a maniac bound by nothing
but her own flesh.
She who slaughters with no regard,
and laughs high
while ending those
who deemed themselves superior
to her beauty.
She, the woman of arrogance
her thoughts
darker than the worst crimes.
Her desires
others' suffering
She is not human.
For
She is the Queen of Insanity.
and the empress of sin

8. The Movements of Pain

What is pain? Is it a tyrant or a saint?
Is it just a teacher,
Wishing to endow us with wisdom
That forever remains?
Or is it the embodiment of tyranny,
Which hurts anyone, anywhere?
Is it pain which crafts the fabric of our humanity,
Or does it wound our soul for its own joy?
Does it shower us in misery
So that joy may be more fulfilling?
Or is it just a menace who wishes
For nothing but sorrow?
What is its creed? What is its purpose?
What has it in store for us mere mortals?
Why does it wish to tear us apart?
Is it just evil?
Then why does it put us back together?
Is it just trying to better us?
Perhaps.
But maybe it heals us
Only to break us once more.
Why does it flutter its wings of misery

And bring sorrow to all?
For in these movements of pain lie
The secrets of humanity.
The question, "Why must there be pain?"
Is simple: it exists to ground us to our mortality.
But the reasons for its severity remain unanswered.
Why is pain so picky?
Why must it wound some
More than others,
Leaving scars upon hearts
That time cannot erase?
Why must it break some
But repair others?
Is pain the creator of value,
Or the destroyer of bonds?
Mere mortals like us
May never know.
For in these movements,
Regrets bind, and sorrow reforms.

9. The Echo of Regret

I walk a thousand paths,
yet none lead home.
I can't find my other half.
Have you lost me?
If you have, then
find me, for
I am the regret which births
your sorrow.
You cannot exist without me,
you still need me,
for I am you.
Find me already.
Was I forgotten? Abandoned?
Will I ever take myself back?
I don't know you, but I know I am you, so answer me:
Is this abyss of thought
yours?
Is it a clue or is it the end?
The cries that once shaped me,
I can't hear them anymore.
Have you moved on?
I drift in the skies of thought,

yet fail to find footing. Have you
turned pure once more?
Where are you?
I am lost.
Please, find me.
Don't let me die.
Without me,
you can't be you.
Where are you?
Return me to your soul.
Let me make you feel once more.
Ahh, I can't remember where you are,
how you looked,
for I am a memory.
But you can remember me, for I am your memory.
My form, your tragedy.
My name, your name.
My purpose, to make you whole.
Remember me.
Don't forget.
Tell me,
Am I still present? Or just a reflection of the past?
Someone tell me—
Which of these paths can take me back?
Which of these million faces is mine?
I have forgotten my other half.
Am I still here?

Please, tell me.
I see you there—
you seem to be me.
I am the missing piece of you?
You see,
I am your regret.
I make you who you are.
I shape your desire.
I am you, after all.
Why do you stand there,
silent and still?
Stop smiling and crying.
Answer me.
You remember me,
don't you? I who haunts you,
who keeps you in darkness.
I just want to help you.
"You are my regret—
a regret I've now forgotten."
Ah, you see through my lies now.
You understand.
I am just a piece of you—
a piece that exists only to cause you pain.
I am nothing more than a memory,
a regret that should fade away.
Now you're going to let me fade,
aren't you?

I am proud of you,
my other half,
for letting me go.
You've learned to counter your own deception.
You've grown.
You've learned to let go of the past
that still haunts you.
Now go find a new "me"—
a "me" of acceptance, not regret.
Make yourself whole again.
For I may have made you miserable,
but I also made you dependable

10. A Facade of Me

The weight of time

erodes my soul.

What's left

is just a facade of what was.

My laughter so fake

It echoes dismay.

My tears so unreal

they have no feel.

In the flow of life,

I have become distant.

My emotions, faint

but I wear them well.

Ahh, my laughter, rehearsed.

My sorrow, coerced.

My actions remain

their reasons, fade.

I no longer

feel the symphony of

my heart.

I no longer see

truth in others joy.

For I am no longer me,

just a mask
wanting to see.

11. Unspoken Solace

Silence It's sometimes a burden,
but other times, an aid.
Some voices of help
could have eased my pain,
but no one ever tried
to touch my soul.
For they thought
my sorrow should only be mine.
The world told them,
men are silent.
And society taught them
that men are fine
on their own.
So they let
me falter in my thoughts,
but failed to see
me breaking.
My only solace
was silence,
my only help,
the void.
I do not know

why the echo of nothing
felt so sincere.
In the silence,
I found hope.
It may be quiet,
but it spoke to me more
than words ever did.

12. The Forsaken One

Adrift in the waves of life,
I search for where I might belong.
All must find their purpose
yet mine slips through every grasp.
I ponder
why no path sings my name.
I wonder
why I decay
amid the rush
of living.
I walk countless roads,
but none let me linger.
No haven calls me home.
Why do the flickers of affection
never bloom into flame?
Why won't hope
shed even a sliver of light for me?
Why am I caged
within the shadows of my own soul?
Why does no hand
reach for mine?
Why does no heart

beat for me?
Am I a man
of no worth,
or a worth unseen?
Why must I be cast aside
used, then forgotten?
Why
must I exist as a doll,
played with and discarded?
My questions echo
into silence.
There are no answers.
Words cannot pave my way.
So I will carve it myself
set my soul alight,
and burn through the dark.
For purpose
is not gifted
it is forged.

13. When Can I Break

When can I break myself
so that I may ease my pain?
When can I let it rain,
so the drops can cleanse my sins?
Why must it all be so painful?
Why am I unable to begin once more?
Why do lies keep on healing,
while truth only cuts deeper?
Let me break.
Let it rain.
Let the white clouds fade.
Let the endless blues take me away.
Stop chaining me to this realm.
When can I reach freedom?
When can I be free of these shackles
of myself?
When can I leave the past
behind?
When?
When can I become
alive once more?
How am I able to continue,

when the past pulls,
drags me deep?
When will I break free of myself?
When will it rain?
When will my tears
free me of myself?
When can I awaken once more?
When can I see my beloved again?
Have they moved on?
When will this slumber end?
When will I finally learn
to release the hollow inside me?
Let me break.
Stop patching my wounds with lies.
I know you are me,
so cut me, wound me with the truth,
so that I may better myself.
Stop fluffing up a world
in carved lies
just stop.
It's enough. Let me break.
Stop telling me it's okay.
Stop comforting me.
Let my scars run wild.
Let my screams reach the heavens,
for after the pain,
I may reach salvation

and awaken as me once more
or a new me.
For the hospital beds may bind,
but I can still feel my beloved's hand
cling on to me.
And for that
and only for that
let me open my eyes.
Let me see the world.
My hands may tremble
when the echoes of the fake lake
are replaced by the horrors of the hospital,
but I don't care for fake perfection
so I arise once more.
My eyes search for
and I see she has stood by me all this time.
And I am glad that she is still here
by my side.
For the lies may comfort
but only the truth can love.

14. The Dread of the Sunrise

The sun rose once more,
Its beauty paInted the sky.
As the sun's rays alIgned,
The bIrds sang theIr song.
I rose not for the beauty
But because I should for my duty.
The lIght and the somber sun
Are not for me to enjoy.

The weIght of lIfe, bound to me by the chaIns of dread,
shrouds the sun and Drags me Into darkness
leavIng me adrIft In the abyss of thoughts
For the sun has rIsen once more,
And another day has begun.
As I hear the symphony
Crafted by the bIrds,
My thoughts fInally begIn to fall Into place.
My purpose urges me to stand up.
I stIll flaIl In the daze of the mornIng.
I ponder about my purpose,

JACOB ELDHO GEORGE

I search for my reasons,
I recollect my memorIes.
the chaIns of dread drag me upwards
yet I keep on fIndIng reasons to resIst
I sway In bed and reallze all these
Days I walked not because I wIshed to,
But because I had to.
I feel a hInt of sorrow and reallze my path
May be forced. Even so, I must walk
Not for joy, but for my purpose.
So, wIth my thoughts fInally coerced, I stand up
Not because I wIsh to,
But because I must
For no matter what these chaIns wIll never let go

15. To Those Who Never Rose

Many walk with dreams,
but only some walk for them.
Everyone is a dreamer
but only a few dare to become doers.
Most fall
without applause
No celebration
No fulfillment
Only silence
They let shadows nest in their hearts
Let regret speak louder than hope
They feared to differ.
Feared to climb
the jagged staircase
of their own desire
Now they haunt themselves.
Some never found the first step
Some climbed, then crumbled
And some never even tried to rise.
Comfort wrapped around them like chains,

and kept their hopes locked in stillness
For without want,
there is no need
So go on
Walk
Crawl
Drag your soul if you must
just keep moving.
Because dreams may come easily
but they are never reached
without a want.
So set fire to
your desire,
and walk
with your hopes held high.

16. Cradle of the Humane

echoes of past dawns
build us to last past the next.
the tunes of sorrow
forging desire in fire's breath.
the paths we tread
are not taken,
but made.
our hearts seek,
and the soul replies
not bound by flesh,
nor shackled by time.
we do not fear death;
we were born in despair
to find a flare in the dark.
why must
a man's birth determine his fate?
why are those crowned in gold,
who shine with light,
the ones who rule
the darkest?
we may return to the ground,
but we still stand above it.

for we bore pain
to reach joy,
our cries for life
will echo
unignored.
we are brittle,
but not broken.
not slaves to fate,
but makers of meaning.
we do not follow
we carve
our way
with blood,
sweat,
and tears.

17. The Truth in Shadow

Shadows are not born of evil
They are forged from despair
when light forgot their names.
For when the sun forsook them
and the moon rejected them,
they found solace in the shades.
The forgotten are not creatures of tyranny,
just mere puppets of darkness.
They are not endowed in sin
they are just puppeteer'd by it.
The world forgot their names,
so they dwelled in evil
that they might linger
a while longer.
Forgotten children
now rise as devils.
For the devil's cry
their tears echo only wrath,
hardened by resentment.
People said:
"They themselves hid from the light."
But they did not hide

they were so long abandoned
that even a bit of light
would turn them to ash.
For the light had forgotten their name.
For time and time again,
the world bid them farewell,
told them to fade away.
So they arose, one with the shadow.
forged in despair,
made of broken memories,
an echo of endless misery.
They were just like the rest,
until the only thing they had left
was the darkness.
We shunned them.
Now they hunt us.
But even so,
do not blame the shadow for its evil.
Blame the cycle of pain that forged it.

18. Judgement Calls

As the symphony of time rings the
bell of death,
the world we claim
is engulfed in flame.
Our stories turned
to ash,
our mortal bodies are torn
apart.
Our souls begin to seek
another land,
for time has called
upon the end.
An end is seeking
everything and everyone.
The fire
takes all our mortal hands have crafted.
The sinful scream,
the faithful pray,
for time has come,
the day of judgement
has arrived.
And on this day, us mere mortals

will enter either
the grace of heaven or the abyss of hell.

19. Death the Gospel

Death What a name.
A mystery no one could tame.
It takes who it pleases
no matter shame,
no matter fame,
for none can appeal its wants
It is the truth
that all must greet.
Death shapes mortality,
carves desire from fear.
For the fear of death
is what makes our wants sincere.
In fear lies
the soul of yearning.
Without death,
we'd be prideful and unlearning
just slobs adrift,
neither dead nor alive,
without a soul void of purpose,
and barely human.
Death is the gospel of time.
He preaches value,

teaches life's prime principle.
For in death,
we do not die
we merely return
to where silence first spoke
and stars forgot to shine

20. Still We Walk

Our paths may wind
through thorns and stone walls
but still we walk.
For life does not wait
it runs along
and we follow
Pain will etch its teachings into us
sin will taunt us
and death will haunt us
Yet still we walk.
Though our
spirits may break
hope is an ember
we carry like a flame
cupped in desire.
Even when we stumble
we will not fall
for the soul has its own will
that keeps us on our feet
When one of us falters
another lends their aid
for our paths

are not parallel
for they intertwine like rivers
falling into the same ocean
Our wills will collide
but our dreams will sing alike
for within these footsteps
lie the symphony
of countless tales,
fading into an endless sea
that goes on forevermore

Author's Notes

1. **Lost Snow,** Here snow represents a person who has passed away. It explores the last stages of grief and the quiet start of acceptance.

2. **The Creed of Sin** explores sin as a living force through a first-person perspective and how it exists within all of us.

3. **The Prayer of the Ashes** tells the tragic tale of Joan of Arc, a 19-year-old girl who led French armies against the British invasion of France, but whom they caught and burned at the stake.

4. **Sworn in Cold** is about how a soldier slowly loses his innocence, illustrated in a first-person perspective.

5. **The Fallen King**: This is based on the famous British legend of King Arthur. It explores his fall from grace, the betrayal by his son, and the sorrow of a king who once sought glory but found only regret.

6. **The Ones Above** is about anti-royalty and rebellion. Loosely inspired by the French Revolution, it speaks of revolution, resistance, and the fight to end tyranny.

7. **The Queen of Insanity** isn't based on any historical figure; it's simply inspired by the yandere stereotype often seen in Japanese media. It explores obsession, madness, and beauty wrapped in chaos.

8. **The Movements of Pain** is a philosophical outlook on the

nature of pain. It reflects on its purpose and attempts to answer the question: Why does pain exist?

9. **The Echo of Regret** explores regret as a fragmented part of oneself and focuses on the conversation between who we are and what we left behind.

10. **A Facade of Me** is about losing touch with your emotions and becoming untrue to yourself, learning to wear a mask of feeling to hide the emptiness within.

11. **Unspoken Solace** is about the comfort found in silence. It explores how, in abandonment, a person may find peace only in the quiet when no one remains.

12. **The Forsaken One** is about a person unseen by the world, searching for purpose until they realize they must forge their own.

13. **When Can I Break** is about a person whose will becomes the strength that helps them awaken from a coma.

14. **The Dread of the Sunrise** is about the pain of living and the weight of existence; the feeling that everything is forced, yet still finding the strength to keep walking.

15. **To Those Who Never Rose** is about walking for one's dreams and how some are unable to take the first step towards them.

16. **Cradle of the Humane** reflects on what it means to be human. It explores how our identity is shaped by pain, choice, and the desire to create meaning beyond fate or circumstance.

17. **The Truth in Shadow** explores how darkness and evil are born from the abandonment and isolation imposed by society.

18. **Judgement Calls** is about the end of the world and the final

reckoning, where all souls, faithful or sinful, must face judgement.

19. **Death the Gospel** explores how mortality itself gives meaning to life and how death forges purpose.

20. **Still We Walk** is about the resilience of humans and how, no matter what, people will always keep moving forward.

Extra Note: These meanings are just the ones I have put forward for my poems, but the beauty of poetry is how dynamic it is. So don't shy away from creating your own interpretations for my work.

Thank You

Thank you for seeing my world and joining me on this escapade through the realm of my poetry.

I hope you enjoyed reading this book as much as I enjoyed writing it.

To everyone who took the time to read this mess of verses—I am truly grateful.

I hope I've inspired you to write your own, because I believe poetry isn't about perfection.

Perfection is just a limit.

And if a 15-year-old kid like me can write poetry, then anyone can.

Poetry is about being dynamic.

It's about finding your own voice and your own way to write.

So, to those who read, felt, or questioned my poetry—

Thank you.

www.ingramcontent.com/pod-product-compliance
Lightning Source LLC
Chambersburg PA
CBHW031241130726
47988CB00008B/3176